THE GRIFFIN POETRY PRIZE
Anthology 2016

Published in Canada in 2016 and in the USA in 2016 by House of Anansi Press Inc.
www.houseofanansi.com

House of Anansi Press is committed to protecting our natural environment.
As part of our efforts, the interior of this book is printed on paper that contains 30% PCW,
is made with windpower, and is acid-free.

18 17 16 15 16   1 2 3 4 5

Library and Archives Canada Cataloguing in Publication

Cataloguing data available from Library and Archives Canada

Cover design: Chloé Griffin and Kyra Griffin
Cover image: Simone's hand, photograph by Chloé Griffin
Inside cover image: artwork by Chloé Griffin
Typesetting: Marijke Friesen

Canada Council **Conseil des Arts**
for the Arts **du Canada**

ONTARIO ARTS COUNCIL
CONSEIL DES ARTS DE L'ONTARIO
an Ontario government agency
un organisme du gouvernement de l'Ontario

*We acknowledge for their financial support of our publishing program
the Canada Council for the Arts, the Ontario Arts Council, and the Government of Canada
through the Canada Book Fund.*

Printed and bound in Canada

THE GRIFFIN POETRY PRIZE

Anthology 2016

A SELECTION OF THE SHORTLIST

Edited by ADAM SOL

2001
Paul Celan (International)
Translated by Heather McHugh
and Nikolai Popov
Anne Carson (Canadian)

2002
Alice Notley (International)
Christian Bök (Canadian)

2003
Paul Muldoon (International)
Margaret Avison (Canadian)

2004
August Kleinzahler
(International)
Anne Simpson (Canadian)

2005
Charles Simic (International)
Roo Borson (Canadian)

2006
Kamau Brathwaite
(International)
Sylvia Legris (Canadian)

2007
Charles Wright (International)
Don McKay (Canadian)

2008
John Ashbery (International)
Robin Blaser (Canadian)

2009
C. D. Wright (International)
A. F. Moritz (Canadian)

2010
Eiléan Ní Chuillieanáin
(International)
Karen Solie (Canadian)

2011
Gjertrud Schnackenberg
(International)
Dionne Brand (Canadian)

2012
David Harsent (International)
Ken Babstock (Canadian)

2013
Ghassan Zaqtan (International)
Translated by Fady Joudah
David W. McFadden (Canadian)

2014
Brenda Hillman (International)
Anne Carson (Canadian)

2015
Michael Longley (International)
Jane Munro (Canadian)

CONTENTS

CANADIAN SHORTLIST

PREFACE

You enter a hall — you've been invited, it's a great honour — filled with singers. Some six hundred people are singing their hearts out in a wide variety of styles. Some are on platforms of their own construction, some face the wall. Some bellow operatically, some whisper into their hands. The sound in the hall is something out of a bird house. Or a train station.

It's your job to clear the room.

There are two categories of singers — Canadian and International. You have been asked to choose the best three Canadians, and the best four Internationals. That means, essentially, that you have to send everyone else out.

You recognize some of the performers. Some are well known in your field. Some are well known in other fields. Some you've admired for years. But you're not there to evaluate their reputations, or your feelings for them. You're trying to evaluate the song they sing. The set of songs they're singing now.

Slowly, hesitantly, you set about your task. At first there are a few singers who are easily weeded out because, whatever the sincerity of their efforts, they do not yet have control of their instruments. You wish them well and send them on their way.

But there aren't as many of those quick exits as you'd hoped. There's something worth listening to in so many. A melody line, a lyric, a style or subject you want to learn more about. And no one is perfect. A young jazz singer with flair and panache who sometimes drifts off-key. A sonorous baritone who can occasionally drone. A master of melisma, but is he occasionally just showing off? What does it mean to choose the best ones? Which criteria should you emphasize?

You have to listen harder, longer, to decide who stays, and who goes. But remember that this is actually part of the pleasure of the experience. You have to admit it, you're enjoying yourself immensely, whatever the pressure. All of this music ricocheting around in the hall, and in your head. Every which way you turn, another talent, another voice.

There are singers whose style and approach are so different from your own that you must strain to access their music. They sing in an unfamiliar tonal scale, but do they sing masterfully in that scale? You are not always sure. But how can you be sure? You must distrust your taste, and then fall back onto your taste, and then distrust it, and so on. You worry that occasionally you're not concentrating as well as you ought to. Your son calls in the middle of one performance to tell you that his bicycle has a flat tire, can you fetch him from school? There are other demands upon your attention. You're not always as good a listener as you'd like to be.

You begin to sense that there are people outside awaiting your decisions. This does nothing to ease the tension.

Fortunately, there are two others in the hall, with the same task that you are struggling with. Their tastes are slightly different, but once you find each other, the partnership helps to ease much of your anxiety and confusion. And thankfully they are both thoughtful, generous, prepared — they point to voices you missed at the first hearing, and they diligently return to singers you are excited about.

Once you've narrowed yourselves down to about two dozen voices, you can really set about listening with a new intensity. This is the best part so far, where you can dig deeper, compare more thoughtfully, relish the artistry of each performance.

There are compromises, negotiations, discussions.

The three of you comfort yourselves with the knowledge that there's no possible way to include every worthy musician on the shortlist you've been asked to choose. It's both a torture and a consolation — there are just too many good singers. Not everyone can reach the shortlist, and only two can win the top prize. It's not your job to provide every good song with the public accolades it deserves — you simply cannot manage it. It's only your job to be sure that the seven singers you *do* choose are worthy of the distinction. And by now, there's no doubt in your minds that the handful remaining — a dozen or so — are all deserving of praise, of attention, of encouragement, and yes, of the financial rewards worthy of their accomplishments.

By the end, the choices are painful, fraught, frustrating, exhilarating. You apologize in your heart to those you must now reluctantly usher out of the hall, and make promises to yourself to return to their work again.

Take a deep breath. Your task is almost complete. With your companions, make the final choices. Stand by them. Bask in their music. Now you can open the doors. Let the celebrations begin.

*

The anthology you hold in your hands is the result of the work that Alice Oswald, Tracy K. Smith, and I pursued, with the impeccable guidance of Ruth Smith and the sponsorship of The Griffin Trust For Excellence In Poetry, from November through May. There were somewhere in the neighbourhood of 630 books of poetry submitted for the prize, and there were days when the task seemed impossible, even ridiculous. But more often, my brain was delightedly swimming with all the artistry heaped upon me. I would arrive at my kids' school to pick them up with one poet in my coat pocket, one poet in my left ear, and another in my right. It was thrilling.

Prizes are an odd way to celebrate poetic accomplishment. One of the reasons we love poetry is because it doesn't have the competitive zero-sum game of other endeavours — Usain Bolt is a champion because he consistently beats everyone else on the track, but we don't have clear markers to judge whether or not Dickinson was better than Whitman, and thankfully we don't have to. We can love them both equally, and differently. On the other hand, if you're reading this anthology, you probably believe, as I do, that artistic excellence should be rewarded as much as possible, and that there are precious few ways to grant poets acknowledgement as magnanimously as the Griffins have created with this prize. It's an imperfect method, with an imperfect process, but if the alternative to imperfect prizes is *no* prizes, I'll stick with imperfection. Personally I feel the same way about governments, love, and life. As Tracy said during our first conference call, we who choose the winners are given the chance to spread some good karma in the world by awarding a few outstanding poets a not-insignificant windfall for their efforts. I feel blessed to have been a part of this good work for 2016.

Adam Sol, April 2016

THE GRIFFIN POETRY PRIZE
Anthology 2016

INTERNATIONAL
SHORTLIST

NORMAN DUBIE

The Quotations of Bone

The poems in Dubie's newest collection are deeply oneiric, governed by vigorous leaping energy that brings the intimate into contact with history, and blurs the distinction between what is real because it once happened, and what is real because of the emphatic manner in which it has been felt. Longtime admirers of Dubie will certainly recognize the familiar mind and spirit able to punch through the surface of experience and into deep psychic quandary with a single revelatory gesture ("Did you ever want to give someone // All your money?") — but that tendency is greatly amplified here. One feels the unconscious mind working ceaselessly, even playfully, alongside memory, imparting the poems as if with a strange and consoling living spirit. This makes for a heightened sense of mystery and mortality in poems of private experience. And when such an impulse is aligned with public history — the division of Germany, say, or the acceleration of the planet's ecological crisis — it is outright haunting. Dubie's uncontested mastery of the lyric poem has, in this collection, broken into strange and revelatory territory.

Prologue Speaking in Tongues

Sitting in the baked boulder field,
Jeremy called it a field of spuds, cactus tuft
rather than shavings of cheddar. The water
was good for this darker incline
of the Superstitions. The Dutchman says
one wing, one rock. You thought
Tagore's dress had a red pleated meridian
just below his breasts.

These holy men who make poems
with oil lamps disfiguring their faces, the nose
cleaved like a dead Venetian's slipper.
The lips
mocking a song of Cole Porter's . . .
easy to love. You said so, pointing
at the desert's full compass
because the world turns its circumference
into pond water's broken
golden mean. Abulafia?

I've refused to anyone say exactly
how, it a death, not the usual cribbage
or begging a difference
in socks . . .   gosh, I said
I do not want to hear it much
was clear of, Jeremy thought,
spuds. As if that could hurt anyone.
But it did.

British Petroleum

for Laura and Danny

A pollen link twisting in wind, the weak
purpling of salt urchins
and the sheath of the sea
itself printing certificates —
it is a malady of time
opposing mass, mass
hastening the gull to the horizon.

A line of Chinese characters
orbiting in ink, the minstrel sleep —
the body of Hart Crane washing up
on a white beach in the Yucatan. Peggy Guggenheim
has scrambled eggs with goat cheese
and there were fresh dates in the muffins.

Yet, he leapt into the gulf in blue
pajamas.

Yet, he leapt into the sea. It is
a classical difficulty for a bird reflected
in water, for water
reflected in the sky bisected
by the gull who plunges into the sea.

It isn't ink
we repeat in ...   It isn't
mollusks whitening beach scree ...
it's the city, it's night ark
gone alphabet with quarks
    entering the impossibly strange intercessional dark.

The Novel as Manuscript

An ars poetica

I remember the death, in Russia,
of postage stamps
like immense museum masterpieces
patchwork
wrapped in linen, tea stained,
with hemp for strapping . . .

these colored stamps designed for foreign places
were even printed during famine —
so when they vanished, so did the whole
Soviet system:
the Berlin Wall, tanks from Afghanistan,
and Ceauşescu's bride before a firing squad.

It had begun with the character of Yuri Zhivago
in a frozen wilderness, the summer house
of his dead in-laws, his
pregnant mistress asleep
before the fireplace
with flames dancing around a broken chair, piano keys,
and the gardener's long black underwear.

Lara lying there. A vulgar fat businessman
coming by sleigh to collect her for the dangers
of a near arctic escape . . .

But for Yuri, not that long ago, he was
with celebrity,
a young doctor publishing a thin volume

of poems in France, he was writing
now at a cold desk
poems against all experience
and for love of a woman buried
in moth-eaten furs on the floor —

while he wrote
wolves out along the green tree line
howled at him. The author of this novel,
Boris Pasternak, arranged it all. Stalin would
have liked to have killed him. But superstition kept him from it.
So, the daughter of Pasternak's mistress eventually
is walking with a candle
through a prison basement —
she is stepping over acres of twisted corpses
hoping to locate her vanished mother . . .
she thinks this reminds her of edging slowly
over the crust on a very deep snow, just a child who believes
she is about to be swallowed by the purity of it all,
like this write your new poems.

Lines for Little Mila

Here, in a cloud of rising flour
she dabs at her chin — aging
leaves a blemish just like this ...
the egg behind the cloud
of flour now falling
to a black mica counter.

Grandmother with a coffee tin
full of raw milk. The sun
gone beyond the mountains
long before it's gone from us.

Men cleaning fish, husking
corn on the porch.

I told a friend's little girl
about some of this,
and she immediately
slumbered, putting
a blue ghost inside my chest.

I said to her —
so you still remember things from the other side?
Then quickly I added —

of that river?

The Quotations of Bone

for Marvin

The meal of bone was a soured milk —
just the heads of giant elk
in a dark circle looking down
on a wooden bowl of soda crackers
and pork. One large knife
resting in the meat
of a woodsman's calloused hand.
He grins at his woman
who is slowly poisoning him
with the stringy resins of morning glory.
A tasteless turpentine with pink pig.
The speeches of bone
are matrimonial in early autumn —
by January there's a froth of blood
at a nostril.
He thinks a long icicle is buried in his ear.
She thinks D. H. Lawrence was a grim buccaneer.
I hate most men. Adore the few named Lou.
One small addendum:
the dead elk are grinning too.

At First Sky in April

In Tehran; in the alleyway of a jail
they're shooting their children
high, in the back of the skull
because, with this approach, less blood
is spilled —   the Russian *cheka*
established this practice in basement showers
where naked aristocrats in endless
lines fell in the cold cascade,
their bodies dragged up coal chutes
to the canvas of idling trucks for the certain passage
to the lime pits of poorly lit suburbs.

At night in these black potato fields,
the *cheka* posted guards to discourage starving dogs —
it was these boys who reported
on the trafficking ghosts even far
back into the stubble of the woods. One kid said
these phantoms looked
like broken kites dragging
along the ground in a fitful wind. There is
something absolutely credible about this account —

I mean, boys, in late March, thinking of kites, boys
with lice,
with their penises flooding with light,
lights tied to their rifle barrels with hemp, *a dog
yelps once, twice . . .*

Under a Tabloid Moon

I

A clear afternoon. Forgive me
like the brass loud horns
against the blinding snow of a hillside.

Cosmo Monkhouse has just begun to deliver
a eulogy over his very own corpse.
And smartly he just said it: *forgive me.*

Drifts of nitrogen
crossing his hallucination of an original savannah
bordered by a yellow swamp.

Basically, again, I will miss you.

II

The kitchen is cold and smelling
of burnt toast. A sweet and sickly odor.
A smell, I thought, like the parallel of baroque
trumpets. A send-off with a landscape you have never
          known. My
vision went cloudy, milk
with the salt of tears. I washed them
in your cold pond water. Laura said

not to let them
fill you with water like a balloon.
So I refused them. Later in the afternoon
you did also.

III
So, friend, you could have died on a prison island
of the Emperor Domitian. The radio
gone silent.
The bridle tack on the locust,
at Patmos, gone gold and black
in a setting sun —

the portal light, on your darkening face,
now, a rose light on a sinking
freighter: thousands of swifts
flying from the rusted bulkheads.

The tabloid newspaper read:
dead, 13 Bengal tigers.

The Mirror

for Richard Howard

We dream of two dragons
conflicted in a wilderness.
It is only the spatial instance
of a luckless accidental order
that says "horse" rather than "house"
but also
says "horse"
rather than "aqueduct."

These, all in the same moment,
spontaneous or
immeasurably meek.
As if under a cloak
of nearness or inevitability
like two suns become one.

It is not belief but
an attraction
to an experience we hunger after,
here and now, an almost
self-annihilating
difference become common, beyond
fear.

If you have changed water to wine,
you will soon
turn wine into tears.

JOY HARJO

Conflict Resolution for Holy Beings

Joy Harjo has been a crucial figure in American letters for decades, and her latest collection, *Conflict Resolution for Holy Beings*, presents her at the height of her powers. Intermingling Mvskoke storytelling, rock-and-roll lyrics, cityscapes, and personal address, Harjo's poems are at once sweeping in their concerns and intimate in their tone and approach. Harjo's is a poetics that is not afraid to speak directly when the moment warrants, nor to refer to traditions — literary traditions, folk traditions, musical traditions — with effortless erudition. *Conflict Resolution for Holy Beings* is a book of transitions and transformations, inhabiting liminal spaces like hotel rooms and deteriorating natural landscapes. The poems urge engagement, but they also encourage a wider perspective, because for Harjo even "the edge between life and death is thinner than a dried animal bladder." In the midst of profound change both personal and global, these poems offer guidance and empathy, ceremony and admonishment, wisdom, comfort, and song.

We Were There When Jazz Was Invented

I have lived 19,404 midnights, some of them in the quaver of
    fish dreams
And some without any memory at all, just the flash of the
    jump
From a night rainbow, to an island of fire and flowers — such
    a holy
Leap between forgetting and jazz. How long has it been
    since I called you back?
After Albuquerque with my baby in diapers on my hip; it
    was a difficult birth,
I was just past girlhood slammed into motherhood. What a
    bear.

Beyond the door of my tongue is a rail and I'm leaning over
    to watch bears
Catch salmon in their teeth. That realm isn't anywhere near
    Los Angeles. If I dream
It all back then I reconstruct that song buried in the muscle
    of urgency. I'm bereft
In the lost nation of debtors. Wey yo hey, wey yo hey yah
    hey. Pepper jumped
And some of us went with him to the stomp. All night,
    beyond midnight, back
Up into the sky, holy.

It was a holy mess, wholly of our folly, drawn of ashes
    around the hole
Of our undoing. Back there the ceremonial fire was
    disassembled, broken and bare, like chord breaks
    forgetting to blossom. Around midnight, I turn my back
And watch prayers take root beneath the moon. Not that
    dreams
Have anything to do with it exactly. I get jumpy
In the aftermath of a disturbed music. I carried that baby up
    the river, gave birth

To nothing but the blues in buckskin and silk. Get back, I
    said, and what bird
Have you chosen to follow in your final years of solitude?
    Go ahead, jump holy
Said the bear prophet. Wey ya hah. Wey ya hah. All the way
    down to the jamming
Flowers and potholes. There has to be a saxophone
    somewhere, some notes bear
Little resemblance to the grown child. Now I've got to be
    dreaming.
Take me back

Or don't take me back to Tulsa. I can only marry the music;
    the outlook's bleak
Without it. I mean it. And then I don't. Too many questions
    mar the answer. Breath
Is the one. And two. And. Dream sweet prophet of sound,
    dream
Mvskoke acrobat of disruption. It's nearing midnight and
    something holy
Is always coming around. Take love for instance, and the
    bare
Perfect neck of a woman who's given up everything for the
    forbidden leap

To your arms as you lean over the railing to hear the music
hopping at the jump
Pull of the line. She will never be here again in the break of
the phrase back
Before this maverick music was invented. It's the midnight
hour and sweet dark love bares
It all. I can hear it again; the blue moon caving in to tears of
muscle and blood. Birth
Of the new day begins less than one second after. It's that
exact, this science of the holy.
So that's where it is, this incubation of broken dreams.

It took forever for that bear of a horn player to negotiate the
impossible jump.
Weh yo hey Weh yo bah, those water spirits will carry that
girl all the way back
To the stomp grounds where jazz was born. It's midnight.
How holy.

Talking With the Sun

I believe in the sun.
In the tangle of human failures of fear, greed, and
    forgetfulness, the sun gives me clarity.
When explorers first encountered my people, they called us
    heathens, sun worshippers.
They didn't understand that the sun is a relative, and
    illuminates our path on this earth.

After dancing all night in a circle we realize that we are a
    part of a larger sense of stars and planets dancing with us
    overhead.
When the sun rises at the apex of the ceremony, we are
    renewed.
There is no mistaking this connection, though Walmart
    might be just down the road.
Humans are vulnerable and rely on the kindnesses of the
    earth and the sun; we exist together in a sacred field of
    meaning.

Our earth is shifting. We can all see it.
I hear from my Inuit and Yupik relatives up north that
    everything has changed. It's so hot; there is not enough
    winter.
Animals are confused. Ice is melting.

The quantum physicists have it right; they are beginning to
    think like Indians: everything is connected dynamically
    at an intimate level.
When you remember this, then the current wobble of the
    earth makes sense. How much more oil can be drained,
Without replacement; without reciprocity?

I walked out of a hotel room just off Times Square at dawn
to find the sun.
It was the fourth morning since the birth of my fourth
granddaughter.
This was the morning I was to present her to the sun, as a
relative, as one of us. It was still dark, overcast as I walked
through Times Square.
I stood beneath a twenty-first century totem pole of symbols
of multinational corporations, made of flash and neon.

The sun rose up over the city but I couldn't see it amidst the
rain.
Though I was not at home, bundling up the baby to carry
her outside,
I carried this newborn girl within the cradleboard of my
heart.
I held her up and presented her to the sun, so she would be
recognized as a relative,
So that she won't forget this connection, this promise,
So that we all remember, the sacredness of life.

Spirit Walking in the Tundra

All the way to Nome, I trace the shadow of the plane as it
  walks
Over turquoise lakes made by late spring breakup
Of the Bering Sea.
The plane is so heavy with cargo load it vibrates our bones.
Like the pressure made by light cracking ice.

Below I see pockets of marrow where seabirds nest.
Mothers are so protective they will dive humans.

I walk from the tarmac and am met by an old friend.
We drive to the launching place
And see walrus hunters set out toward the sea.
We swing to the summer camps where seal hangs on drying
  frames.
She takes me home.
I watch her son play video games on break from the
  university.

This is what it feels like, says her son, as we walk up tundra,
Toward a herd of musk ox, *when you spirit walk.*
There is a shaking, and then you are in mystery.

Little purple flowers come up from the permafrost.
A newborn musk ox staggers around its mother's legs.

I smell the approach of someone with clean thoughts.
She is wearing designs like flowers, and a fur of ice.
She carries a basket and digging implements.
Her smell is sweet like blossoms coming up through the
  snow.
The spirit of the tundra stands with us, and we collect
  sunlight together,
We are refreshed by small winds.

We do not need history in books to tell us who we are
Or where we come from, I remind him.
Up here, we are near the opening in the Earth's head, the
    place where the spirit leaves and returns.
Up here, the edge between life and death is thinner than
    dried animal bladder.

(FOR ANUQSRAAQ AND QITUVITUAQ)
NOME, ALASKA, 2011

Midnight is a horn player warmed up tight for the last set. One a.m. is a drummer who knows how to lay it sweet. Two a.m. is a guitar player who is down on his luck. Three a.m. is a bass player walking the floor crazy for you. Four a.m. is a singer in silk who will do anything for love. Five a.m. is kept for the birds. Six a.m. is the cleaning crew smoking cigarettes while they wait for the door to open. Seven a.m. we're having breakfast together at the diner that never closes. Eight a.m. and we shut it down, though the clock keeps running, all through the town.

Charlie and the Baby

Charlie was in Venice, wheeling his granddaughter in a
   stroller
Down the boardwalk, through noisy spring crowds.
He was the happiest he'd ever been. He was with the baby,
The sun, and the ocean who busied herself carrying time
And breaking it against sand.

In the sky over Charlie and the baby were flights coming in
   from Hawaii, China, and other lands.
They circled like reachable stars.
Men fished from the pier; mothers unfolded picnics,
As children played hide-and-seek.
In the blue breathed immense light beings.
From their eyes, we were lost and small.

Charlie called and asked me how I was doing —

I probably recited the usual, you know: I am living a life
That takes me almost everywhere. Jet lag. Band practice.
   The kids. Poems.

Charlie was weary with the poverty of making a living of
   comedy.
(We laughed.)
I could smell sea-riding wind, could hear the baby's laughter.

New plants were growing from the grief of my mother's
   recent death.
(We listened.)
As for poets, I said, it's about the same.

We talked what we always talked:
History, saxophones, kids, words, Floyd, Buffy, Jennifer Jesus,
    healing, airplanes, Floyd, prayers, philosophy, Indians,
    Indians, and why we're in the predicament we're in.

Every word that's ever said tries to find a way to live.

You're gone now, and I'm still in this predicament called
    living, Charlie.
I imagine things don't change much when you cross the line.
You're still you.
And I'm still here at the other end of this long, long wave,
    listening.

Sunrise

Sunrise, as you enter the houses of everyone here, find us.
We've been crashing for days, or has it been years.
Find us, beneath the shadow of this yearning mountain,
    crying here.
We have been sick with sour longings, and the jangling of
    fears.
Our spirits rise up in the dark, because they hear,
Doves in cottonwoods calling forth the sun.
We struggled with a monster and lost.
Our bodies were tossed in the pile of kill. We rotted there.
We were ashamed and we told ourselves for a thousand
    years,
We didn't deserve anything but this —
And one day, in relentless eternity, our spirits discerned
    movement of prayers
Carried toward the sun.
And this morning we are able to stand with all the rest
And welcome you here.
We move with the lightness of being, and we will go
Where there's a place for us.

DON PATERSON

40 Sonnets

About half the poems in Don Paterson's latest book are
strict sonnets and half are wild or disobedient sonnets
(four beats to a line, one word to a line, one word to a
whole poem or sometimes just plain prose) but these vari-
ants of one form work together to make a fascinating and
sustained piece of music, like a fugue. The poems use their
patterns to think through questions about consciousness.
They are smart and exact but at the same time surprisingly
emotional. Since 1993 Paterson has been eroding his style
from the light loose poems of *Nil Nil* towards the spare,
almost mathematical brilliance of this book. He can write
now with resonant clarity about anything: his dog, his
children, the air, Dundee Council, Tony Blair, the soul.
The melody of the sonnet form gives all these subjects an
unstrained seriousness. *40 Sonnets* is a wonderful offering,
patiently made.

Wave

For months I'd moved across the open water
like a wheel under its skin, a frictionless
and by then almost wholly abstract matter
with nothing in my head beyond the bliss
of my own breaking, how the long foreshore
would hear my full confession, and I'd drain
into the shale till I was filtered pure.
There was no way to tell on that bare plain
but I felt my power run down with the miles
and by the time I saw the scattered sails,
the painted front and children on the pier
I was nothing but a fold in her blue gown
and knew I was already in the clear.
I hit the beach and swept away the town.

Lacrima

For years, I'd begged him for the smallest word.
Finally I cursed him with the worst I knew.
Silent skies. Maybe it was true,
and he never was? But then I heard
his breath behind my own; even in his sleep
he brooded on the form my hell might take.
So I forgave him. O that shook him awake —
he raged and howled ; then he began to weep.

One drop belled at the fracture in his side,
and then a stream, a flood, a tidal race —
all he was was one huge tear. In his place
there stood a human shape cut from the void,
an empty tearless glory. I walked in
and now I wear it like a second skin.

Francesca Woodman

i

At the heart there is a hollow sun
by which we are constructed and undone

ii

Behind the mirror. Favourite place to hide.
I didn't breathe. They looked so long I died.

iii

What's shown when we unveil, disclose, undress,
is first the promise, then its emptiness

iv

Ghost-face. Not because I turned my head.
but because what looked at me was dead.

v

— We don't exist — We only dream we're here —
This means we never die — We disappear —

vi

We'd met 'in previous lives', he was convinced.
Yeah, I thought. And haven't spoken since.

vii

All rooms will hide you, if you stand just so.
All ghosts know this. That's really all they know.

The Version

after Nicanor Parra

Like many of my colleagues, I too received the envelope of dark green card bearing the green-and-gold stamp of their far-off land, and the handwritten invitation to contribute a new poem to be translated for the five-hundredth edition of their journal, which would contain nothing but foreign poets in translation. The Slovenian business was still fresh in my memory, and I'd rather have hacked off my hand at the wrist than see my work diminished in that manner again. But the mortgage payment was looming, and their line-rate was impossibly generous . . . So I conceived of a brilliant plan. I would write a poem *about* translation, designed to lose precisely *everything* in translation — such would be the density of its idiom, the baroque recursion of its argument, the depth of its lyric intrigue. (Its subject, or at least such part of it as could be paraphrased, was the creation of a poem so volatile it would burst spontaneously into flames before it could be read.) 'The Version' would consist of my biographical note and photograph, opposite a blank recto carrying only an apology from the editor. My notoriety would be instantaneous. I daydreamed . . . From that day, I would be known in their land as 'The Silent Poet' . . . My blank books would be set texts at their universities, and I would be flown to their stadia to not read to thousands. I sent off my only copy of the work, with a firm request that they destroy the original after the translation was made, for The Silent Poet leaves no trace. As I'd predicted, a succession of their own poets ducked out of the task, claiming everything from migraine to the sudden deaths of close family members. But rather than give up, they passed it on to some professor of Stylistics. Being one of those smartasses whose game is to make something of anything — of absolutely nothing, if necessary — it seems he read my barely moving lips, and drew his conclusions. (Whether he had intended to honour my request to shred the original or not is irrelevant: we can assume my poem was lost when a flunked student of his turned arsonist, and razed his house to the ground.) When they sent me my author's copy of the journal — assuming, correctly, that I did not know one word of their raucous, glide- and liquid-free tongue — they thought 'I might be interested to know' what their man had made of it.

I ascertained that this reverse translation had been made by some chap who mostly worked on software manuals. The rendering as prose and consequent loss of my immaculate alexandrines I could have foreseen, but as far as I could recall, my original sonnet bore no relation to this poem in any way whatsoever. However, what animated me most at the time — I now find this hilarious — was its facile *mise en abîme*, and its rather blokey and ludic tone, given I'd quit doing that sort of thing fifteen years ago. And then the real horror began. A friend alerted me to the fact that someone had submitted this garrulous bullshit to some magazine *in my name*. When I wrote to the editor to protest, she angrily referred me to three other journals where 'The Version' had *also* appeared, each time in a completely different form: one is violently pornographic, and directs the reader towards a number of illegal sites on the dark web; another accuses (in virulently anti-Semitic terms) another poet, by name, of fucking his own sister; another yields an acrostic insulting the prophet Mohamed . . . My increasingly hysterical protestations fall on deaf ears. Within a week, I hear that I have been dropped from several reading lists, that a Nobel laureate is suing me for plagiarism, that a series of public readings has been cancelled . . . Now my work is returned from journals unopened, my agent has dropped me, and yesterday I received an email from my publisher saying *under the current circumstances we cannot in all conscience continue to support your work.* While I dwindle, 'The Version' proliferates. I am writing this in the cupboard below the stairs, and the banging on the front door has stopped; I think they are in the house now. A yard away, a man with a voice I half know has just spoken my name. I cannot let him hear me breathe.

Requests

O tell us more about your dad,
or why your second wife went mad,
or how it was you had no choice
but to give those men a voice;
sing that Cornish lullaby
you hush your kids with when they cry,
produce a boiled egg from your pocket,
a flageolet from your jacket,
expand on your idea that rhyme
is dead, or tell us of the time
you dropped your cellphone in the toilet;
a joke, a bird-call — please don't spoil it,
go on with your brilliant proem!
Anything but read your poem.

For a Drowned Poet

after Du Fu

An October wind
has cleared the sky

and the brown waters
clarify their depths.

What might one reflect
in this empty hour?

When will the wild geese
bring their high word?

I whisper with one
fool enough to choose

perfection of the work.
How hell rejoiced.

I mail this poem for him
into the river.

Mercies

She might have had months left of her dog-years
but to be who? She'd grown light as a nest
and spent the whole day under her long ears
listening to the bad radio in her breast.
On the steel bench, knowing what was taking shape
she tried and tried to stand, as if to sign
that she was still of use, and should escape
our selection. So I turned her face to mine,
and seeing only love there — which, for all
the wolf in her, she knew as well as we did —
she lay back down and let the needle enter.
And love was surely what her eyes conceded
as her stare grew hard, and one bright aerial
quit making its report back to the centre.

The Roundabout

For Jamie and Russ

It's moving still, that wooden roundabout
we found at the field's end, sunk in the grass
like an ancient buckler from the giants' war.
The first day of good weather, our first out
after me and your mother. Its thrawn mass
was like trying to push a tree over, or row
a galley sealed in ice. I was all for
giving up when we felt it give, and go.
What had saved the axle all those years?
It let out one great drawn-out yawn and swung
away like a hundred gates. Our hands still burning
we lay and looked up at a sky so clear
there was nothing in the world to prove our turning
but our light heads, and the wind's lung.

ROWAN RICARDO PHILLIPS

Heaven

Rowan Ricardo Phillips's second collection of poems pushes off from his debut, *The Ground*, by looking out and off toward the many Heavens we find in our midst: the heaven of the natural world, large and silent and sublime; the heaven of ecstatic language and lyric possibility; the heavens of memory and of love; the flawed, finite, deeply familiar heaven of the 21st Century. In poems of exquisite craft, rich allusion, and nimble intelligence, Phillips creates a gathering ground for glimmers of Homer and Shakespeare, Frost and Stevens. But he casts a wide net, also making surprising use of sources as unlikely as the Wu-Tang Clan and Mel Gibson, and as chastening as the recent preponderance of shootings that have left unarmed blacks dead and their assailants deemed "Not Guilty." This is a book that manages to make something indelible of what we've wrought and lost, and of what we are still desperate to decipher — the truth we'll only know from learning to "squint in its direction and poke."

Kingdom Come

Not knowing the difference between Heaven
And Paradise, he called them both Heaven.
So when he shrugged at the thought of a god
Blanched in the lights of implausible heights,
Thumbing the armrests of a throne, that was
Heaven. And when he stared out at the sea,
Feeling familiar to himself at last,
He called that Heaven, too. And nothing changed
About either Paradise or Heaven
For it: Paradise retained its earthen
Glamour; and Heaven, because it can't stand
For anything on its own, like the color
Of rice or a bomb, was happy to play
Along, was happy just to be happy
For once, and not an excuse for mayhem.

Little Song

Both guitars run trebly. One noodles
Over a groove. The other slushes chords.
Then they switch. It's quite an earnest affair.
They close my eyes. I close their eyes. A horn
Blares its inner air to brass. A girl shakes
Her ass. Some dude does the same. The music's
Gone moot. Who doesn't love it when the bass
Doesn't hide? When you can feel the trumpet peel
Old oil and spit from deep down the empty
Pit of a note or none or few? So don't
Give up on it yet: the scenario.
You know that it's just as tired of you
As you are of it. Still, there's much more to it
Than that. It does not not get you quite wrong.

Measure for Measure

Alone in Woody Creek, Colorado,
I fell asleep reading *Measure for Measure,*
Right at the part where the Duke delivers
His Old Testament decision of haste
Paying for haste, and leisure answering
Leisure, like quitting like, and (wait for it)
Measure for measure. I saw it performed
Once, in Stratford; I was maybe twenty.
I only remembered the "measure still
For measure" part, until now. It stuck
With me. But the rest of it was wiped clean
From my memory; all of Stratford, too.
Still, the way the actor leaned on that half
Line, "measure *still* for measure," as though it
Were the measure of his self, measure still
For measure, all these years, I remembered
Being the heart of the play, its great gist;
But I forgot it was a death sentence.
Whether Angelo deserved such a fate,
Or Isabella's ability to
Rise above the mire, doesn't matter:
Death, not beauty, woke me.
                                My neck aches.
All of Shakespeare feels like lead on my chest,
Not for death, let's face it, death awaits us,
Usually with less prescient language,
But death measures us with a noun's contempt
For our imagination, being death
But not dying, making do, like when I
Turn from the Bard, look outside, and behold
A herd of a hundred elk, surviving
The snow as they know how — being elk;
An hour ago they were in the hills,
But now they graze a mere five feet away,

Their world othered by these austere windows;
The massive seven-pointer, chin held high
To prevent his thick neck from crashing down,
Hoofs the snow and starts towards me, but then turns
To compass the valley between his horns.

Lucas and Mark

I sit sandwiched between two Chuck Closes:
Luckless "Lucas," made up of small fat dots
Bursting against black-backgrounded colors,
His unkempt hair, unkempt beard, unkempt stare
Shot past the small bench between him and "Mark."
No one in the Met has ever looked more eager
To be at the Met than "Mark." Every pore
And razor scrape happens. His bucktoothed grin,
His out-of-focus neck and shoulders share
The running joke of being real with us.
Like Buscemi he is a look of love.
His union-grade plastic frames reflect lights
He alone sees. And now, in twos and threes,
Fans pose with "Mark"'s huge head — the Italian
Girls, bronzed in expensive peasant dresses,
Throw up peace signs and then blow him kisses.
— Meanwhile, "Lucas," left alone to brood
On his side of the room, where he is real
From a distance, instead of the crazed pixels
He's revealed to be up close, drops his eyes
Onto me, as though he knows I'm watching
And hopes I know that he's really a man.

The Beatitudes of Malibu

I

Walking across the PCH, we looked
Up and saw, big as the butt of a pen,
Jupiter, fat with light and unheighted.
I looked back at the waiting traffic stalled
At the seaside road's salt-rimmed traffic lights
As they swayed to the Pacific's not-quite-
Anapestic song of sea and air —
The raw and sudden crick of crickets —
The cars, suddenly silent as cows —
And blue Malibu blackening like a bee.

II

A poem is a view of the Pacific
And the Pacific, and the Pacific
Taking in its view of the Pacific,
And the Pacific as the Pacific
(Just like that: as though there's no Pacific)
Ends. A poem is the palm of the ocean,
Closing. It or she or he is merely,
Which means it or she or he is a mar.
But a mar made up of temperament and
Tempo — the red weather in the heart.

III

I'm about to get this all wrong, I know:
Santa Monica behind me, the ocean
To my left, Jupiter high above me,
And Malibu somewhere in my mind, flecked
With mist and dusk and Dylan and strange grays
In the sunsets that stripe the seaside hills
Like the tricolor of a country made
Of beauty, the dream of beauty, and smog.
Sadly, in my mind it's always snowing;
Which is beautiful but austere, unlike here.

IV

Along the thin pedestrian passage
Beside the PCH, just off Sunset,
Mel Gibson chants of beginnings and ends
And lies and facts — Jews and blacks being
Both the lies and facts. His face is ruddy
Like bruschetta. He storms at the police
Because fuck them. He's wearing his T-shirt
Like a toga. He schools them his toga
Wisdom from toga times. He offers them
His toga. They offer him a ride —.

V

Arun's car carried us like metaphor
In a poem or painting; moving meaning;
Moving the current; being the current;
The terse tug of tides: still the great glamour;
Still, even as we speed on the 110,
The music in my head, the Jupiter
Of the mind's unstemmed Pacific Ocean
As it unfurls in the vapor trail of
Malibu, fragrant in far-off fluorescents,
Like a nocturnal flower calling you.

VI

Then Downtown LA and LA Live surged
Up, like marginalia on a newly
Turned page, spangled with bland suggestions,
Fiery accusations of its own
Brilliance that descend into indifference.
We speed nearer and it grows. We veer and
It grows. We park and it grows. Close your eyes.
Now look. And it has grown. Yo la quiero.
But I should know better, if just because
You can smell the injustice in the air.

VII

The Pacific encircles me. Slowly.
As though it doesn't trust me. Or, better
Said, I only understand it this way:
By feeling like a stranger at its blue
Door. The poet with the sea stuck in his
Enjambments can't call out to some Cathay
As though some Cathay exists and be glad.
No, the differences we have should be felt
And made, through that feeling, an eclipsed lack;
A power to take in what you can't take back.

VIII

The old hocus of this ocean's focus
On pulling its waves over the soft surf
Like a skin pulled down tight over the top
Of a drum was, to her, a new hocus.
We stared out with her, out towards Hokusai's
Tiny boats and rising lace-fringed sea swells
No chunk of haiku could think to charter.
It was like the eighth day of creation
In the eighth line of a poem — she sang,
She didn't sing, the sea sang, then stopped.

The Once and Future King of Ohio

Dawn. Two roosters stud the side of the road.
One of them is dead. The other stands there
Stiff in the car's sudden breeze, staring out
Across the hilly Ohio highway,
Skyward towards that something slight of bright
Reds and pinks, a pallid rooster-feathered
Hue, as silent as the rooster standing
And as distant as the rooster on its side.
We drove by, my guide and I, too quickly
To know if one rooster was waiting for
The other, or which had been waiting —,
Or if they'd planned to cross the road together
When suddenly something went terribly wrong,
Either at the end of having crossed it
Or simply, as happens, during the wait.

The whole Ohio highway seemed to know, though,
Like the gate of Heaven you see at death
(As a light or a shining shunning darkness)
Knows Heaven without actually being
Heaven, being rather just a border,
Still part of our plausible world
Of parts, living and dead, male and female,
Color and color, belief and belief . . .
There's really no reason to believe or
Not to believe what you see when you see it.
But when at speed I saw those two roosters
Trying to figure out what's next for them
As the distances we traveled on the
661 swallowed them whole with wheat,
I looked from my passenger's seat into
The car's rearview mirror, and saw nothing
That was neither Heaven nor Ohio

As the horses stirred, and the steeples slept,
And the state flattened out like a mirror.
And am I not a mirror for that mirror?

CANADIAN

SHORTLIST

PER BRASK AND PATRICK FRIESEN

TRANSLATED FROM THE DANISH WRITTEN BY ULRIKKA S. GERNES

Frayed Opus for Strings & Wind Instruments

This collaboration between Danish poet Ulrikka Gernes and Canadian writers Brask and Friesen, is astonishingly successful, every line at home in its new language. The poems have not stopped being poems. In fact, now that they are speaking through three mouths (one female, two male) they seem to have gathered an extra layer of strangeness which suits their dream-like, mutable, almost anonymous voice: "Since then I have been standing in the subway singing to passersby and nobody knows my name . . ." The world of the poems is twilit, borderless, melancholy, associative, seeping; and these qualities are carried over from the imagery into the fluid, blended structures of the verse. Full of arresting detail and quiet everyday language, this is the second Gernes book to be translated by these writers and it is masterful.

A Frayed Opus for Strings

and wind instruments
and a lit bicycle shed
in the backyard; all that desire
constrained in shuddering
apartment blocks from where
my mind wanders
on daylong steep mountain paths
only to curl up
against your sleeping back
on a bespoken globe.

Night-Black Silver, January's Luminous

morning-darkness leaves behind its blacking,
rubbing off on everything I touch.
It could be worse, it could
always be worse, but could it
be better? No, never better than
this moment, it's perfect, it'll never
come back. The child sleeps,
the cat plays with its tail, traffic
sighs past on Falkoner Allé. I jot this down
in the margin of the newspaper, drink
a cup of tea, somewhere someone
opens a book, the year has just begun,
and life, the late dawn sneaks in,
polishes the dark spots clean.

K Was Supposed to Come With the Key, I Was
to wait outside the gate. I arrived on time,
the time we had agreed on and waited, as agreed,
outside the gate. I waited a long time, waited
and waited, waited a very long time. I stood
next to the security guard from Securitas, who also
stood outside the gate. I waited, the security guard from
Securitas just stood there, he wasn't waiting,
it was his job to stand there, he didn't take
any breaks, he just stood there, keeping an eye
on what he was supposed to keep an eye on. K
didn't show up. I waited. When the security guard
from Securitas finished his shift I went home
with him, sat down across from him at the kitchen
table, ate spicy meatballs on rice, summer cabbage
followed by green tea and mango from Brazil.
In the night he laid his human hand between
my shoulder blades before we both stumbled
across the threshold into a brand new now.

Barely Five Minutes Later We've Moved Into
a seven-bedroom apartment on Rosenborggade
with exposed collar beams and rafters
of Pomeranian pine which make the whole construction
visible for anyone to see; the dimensions of a brick
are made to fit a man's hand, door handles and hasps,
fleeting caresses, crisp stucco, look, it matches
my dress; tightly veined wooden floors sated with resin,
those eye-like knots have dried their tears long ago
and all the details about piping and drainage systems
that you have no desire to know are loosing themselves
in the whoosh of an extinct forest, a distant sigh
from Galicia's giant trees flows through the rooms;
I do believe I perceive animal paths twisting through
the thicket of our kisses, wondering whether you too
sense those shadows passing by, shaggy, vigilant,
but with no hesitation about direction or aim,
the scent tears slightly in my nostrils;
you're right: there's more between heaven and earth
than flesh and blood, and I, who never favoured
timber frame, am able all at once to gloss over
your escapades; the raft that carries me across
the rapids is built of longing; no stronger timber
exists and it floats just as easily as it burns.

I Have to Find F. I Don't Know Why And I Don't Know
where, but if I find F I'll get the answer to an important
question. I don't know the question, but at some
point I'll be told. It's something to do with an
envelope. And a parrot feather. I'm in London.
I have a photo of an English row house, the kind of house
there are a million of in London. I have no address.
I only know that it's in London and that F is in the house
in the photo. I must find that house. I have two large
suitcases that are very heavy. In addition I have a rucksack
on my back. It too is heavy. I can barely carry my luggage.
I also have a dog. A small, black and white dog which is
very lively. I have it on a leash but it constantly runs
away from me. Its name is Ziggy. I call and call after it.
It leaps and jumps and barks. It's impossible to control it.
We walk through dark, narrow passages and alleys that
dead-end and we have to walk back. It seems hopeless,
but I mustn't give up. I yell and yell after the dog that
constantly skips away from me. In my pocket I have
the photo of the house, I have to stop continually, put
the suitcases down, take the photo from my pocket
and compare the house in the photo with the houses
we pass. In this way seventeen years go by.

I Write This On the Back of a Turquoise-Blue
coastline, make an X, wishing you were here,
where my body has washed ashore. I'm with you
as a thought this morning. The letter slot
clangs, you bend down, pick up the picture from
the doormat, unshaven, in a bathrobe; tilting your
head you wonder at the colour of the ocean,
an upside-down sky, the clarity of the water,
as though it were impossible to drown.

In the Thicket of Possibilities I Choose The Continental
shelf as my ford, find foothold, take off, firmly determined
to fall in with the spirit of the place, but in vain; I tumble
flopping through the mesh in the net; in the broom closet I have
the company of some rat-like creatures, one of them maintains
it has found the Northwest Passage, possibly just a polite excuse
to make conversation; later on, none of us have been there before,
the dinner party continues and the guests are served baked apples
with licorice meringue, my dinner partner is missing the tip
of his left thumb, I pretend I haven't noticed a thing, fall
in love with lightning speed the moment the guard takes
a nap at the floodgate, always this desire to fill a void, to fit
my body into the shape of someone else's solitude, and the
answers whirring in the air search for questions far too close
to the candles' nervous flames; tonight all men are my husband,
all women his wife, I'm no one's daughter, no one's sister,
no one's mother, anyone can see that my face has travelled, air
hostess, I reply, when anyone queries, I feel dizzy and leave
early, the long haul to Shanghai my excuse.

On H. C. Andersen Boulevard During Rush Hour

around five o'clock I'm a speck of stardust on a bicycle
wrapped in my life's nanosecond, my life's nanosecond,
my life's nanosecond and this poem that doesn't really
fit in anywhere either, and I have already wasted an infinitely
immeasurable fraction of the light intended for me, as I just
manage to glimpse the wing tip of a herring gull tear
a white cut into the air above Langebro, a tear in the blue
and there you are and there's my daughter, the strings, the wind
instruments, a tiny stage and a fragile ship ascending on
the waving pillar of smoke from a cigarette someone
tosses and butts right now under the heel against a flagstone
in the universe and a bleeding cut on the lip screams,
have I loved, have I loved, have I loved enough.

No More Now. Even Fear Has Fear. Even Of Itself.
I refuse to be lonely. No longer. It's enough now.
Language contradicts itself, constantly producing
additions, disclaimers and footnotes. And the body
never gets ready, nails grow out, and hair, in the strangest
places. Here the mountainside is black with lemons.
At the very moment I rest within my contour a dam
breaks. Maybe there's a connection. I am someone
who . . . bounded by skin, is alone. I say it again, as loud
as I can: not another word! Maybe everything is connected.
Several thousand kilometers away you move your hand.
And here everything is instantly flooded.

LIZ HOWARD

Infinite Citizen of the Shaking Tent

With penetrating intelligence and playful musicality, Liz Howard's ambitious debut collection keeps us delightfully off-balance with its mix of lyricism and experiment, allusion and invention. In her efforts "to dream a science that would name me," Howard explores a dizzying array of texts and landscapes, from Dante to Erin Mouré, from logging camps to high school dances. But for a poet so attuned to the self as "a fictive province," we are all "infinite citizens," constructed of dredged materials and fraught histories. Howard is capable of thrilling leaps of language, repurposing Longfellow's *Song of Hiawatha* or imagining an oddly tender childhood memory of a "boreal swing" made from the carcass of a moose. These poems are filled with energy and magic, suspended between competing inheritances, at home in their hyper-modern hybridity. *Infinite Citizen of the Shaking Tent* confronts its legacies with vivid imagery and crackling language, and introduces us to a bold, original poetic voice.

Boreal Swing

My mother hunted moose
as a child my grandfather taught her
how to field dress a bull:
make an incision from the throat
to the pelvis
the abdominal cavity emptied
haul him up between two pines
the body inverted
antlers almost grazing
the soil
each hind limb leashed to a trunk above
to allow the flesh to cool
then she'd climb inside
the open chest
fix her toes along the ledge
of two ribs
and with a kick to the bull's left shoulder
he sent her
swinging

Standard Time

The total psychic economy shimmers
a latent mouthpiece of maple out in the field
anthropologically, this voice in its hollow

All night the blood moon measures the dilation
of your pupil, pinprick or dinner plate
in this plenum where our attention fails to die

A positive outcome, music in the unfinished
basement, a purple curfew for causation, the reply
a sinuous window of dried moths over the harbour

Exercise in temperament pitched back over
the clouded bathroom mirror transiting near to silver
almost female in a song of Velcro afterbirth and gravel

In our settler dreams Plexiglas teeth were stuck in the hide
of the ravine, a freeway of copper wire and sugar bush
metabolics, Copernican limbs, mercury in the water

Little silver pills tracing a path through the lake bed
of submerged logs to a trap of currents under rock
all our odd love and petrochemicals

Not otherwise
specified.

A Wake

Your eyes open the night's slow static at a loss
to explain this place you've returned to from above;
cedar along a broken shore, twisting in a wake of fog.

I've lived in rooms with others, of no place and no mind
trying to bind a self inside the contagion of words while
your eyes open the night's slow static. At a loss

to understand all that I cannot say, as if you came
upon the infinite simply by thinking and it was
a shore of broken cedar twisting in a wake of fog.

If I moan from an animal throat it is in hope you
will return to me what I lost learning to speak.
Your eyes open the night's slow static at a loss

to ever know the true terminus of doubt, the limits of skin.
As long as you hold me I am doubled from without and within:
a wake of fog unbroken, a shore of twisted cedar.

I will press myself into potential, into your breath,
and maybe what was lost will return in sleep once I see
your eyes open into the night's slow static, at a loss.
Broken on a shore of cedar. We twist in a wake of fog.

Debarker

I just want to go back
into the bush and eat
more blueberries
growing wild as she
drops me off at the lumber
mill I'm fifteen and a janitor
cleaning out the urinals
at the debarker I find
pubic hair the lumberjacks
have left long barbs curled
to "put me in my place"
debarker: where they
keep the machine that
cuts the bark away from
the trees years ago my
blood cousin fell in
and emerged skinless
that was before this brain
sprouted from my spine
in an allegory trees
would be distributed
evenly throughout the
narrative in a gesture
of looking back over
my shoulder as mom
pulls away from the
yard I have on a hard
hat that is orange and too

Henceforth, Through the Forest

What auspice will lend me a sacred belt?
northwind skyping
the real of consumer goods

asleep
and cumbrous
all nations in a night
terror

that's a bear
on the porch pawing
at the screen door
for meat

I wrap around this neck
a stolen show of courage
on the summit

maw plied with mosses
spotted grey and earthen
I evacuate them with red nails
before calling it a day

in a fluid movement
I remove my belt
and snap it

at the stakeholders of the commonplace
at a crucifix
at the tariff of longing
at the dawn
at my own name

heavy breathing
the hour was a body scan
and I will be as loud
as I need to

LOLing
in the middle
of mere existence
in the throes
of mystery

a thing
with claws

Bigger Than

Level spread
the lake my bosom
and its shadow

exaltation lifted
my liquid features
from the corroded mist

I have as much at stake
in speaking this
as the water

which also
discloses futurity
in a little black dress

for all history
awaited you
was open to you
bade you
entrance

to an unequivocal buffet
of redacted mischief
we're just friends

hanging out
in my apartment
until the world ends

and now that the world
has ended and we have not ascended
into heaven

here comes the future

let it in
let it in and let
our consumptive prom
begin

North By South

was as if I really knew
but then the dream changed
stalactites under Mexico

become the show
ponies of our thrownness
gradually turning

into an estuary of blood and soy
bless it, unfettered
the open stone's face

there are more totem
moments where the stars
have drunk the ocean

on a self-similar
confessional flight path over
the northern hemisphere

this account of light
as an acquired characteristic
became propositional

just as every forest
would come to speak to us
as a verb

Sweet citizen, I know you
as I know myself: a fictive province
of selves within
doppler range

SORAYA PEERBAYE

Tell: poems for a girlhood

Harrowing and deeply empathetic, *Tell: poems for a girlhood* traces the events surrounding the 1997 murder of teenager Reena Virk by a group of high school class-mates. Peerbaye bears brave witness to the unspeakable brutality of these events, drawing from testimonies of the convicted, the victim's autopsy report, and a history of the landscape itself. And yet, the power of this book derives only partly from the unbearable facts of violence, hatred, and alienation. The true miracle of *Tell* is not merely its choice to sing of such things, but its ability to sing in such a way as to urge the reader to embrace painful sympathies. Peerbaye's language becomes a vehicle not just for exploring what others in the world may be capable of, but also for drawing readers into excruciating proximity with our own adolescent longing, fear, shame, and rage.

Trials

Magnolias in bloom, each trial held in early spring.
Pink-white curve of petals like skinned knees.
Newspapers opened to her eighth grade photograph:
black curls, bronze smile, heirloom gold earring.

In the courtroom, articles of clothing suggested her.
Exhibits. Out of the pleather jacket her torso emerged;
out of her clog boots, her stance. She believed in this,
that her body could be enough. As a girl, I would have liked
to be like that, to have her daring. Still — hard to say,
if I'd have been her friend — her ardour, pungent, dangerous.

Even flowers are ranked, said the woman watching
the proceedings with me. *Roses are worth more
than daisies. Lilies more than daffodils.* I want
her body to stand, be its own testimony. Instead
it's the jacket, held before the witness,
          open, declarative,

while the fair-haired girl behind Plexiglas
says nothing.

Autopsy

1.

    The way certain things could be hidden

by darker skin, the heaviness of hair
        on the body.

    Immersion too
            makes surface bruises
       more difficult to see.

2.
The smallest injuries, first:

        chatter marks
     fingernails crossing
            scraping up
little bits of skin
               then skipping down.

3.

    A burn mark between the eyebrows

the ulcerated

            punched-out shape
    consistent
      with a cigarette.

4.

Bloody discharge from the nose . . .
bruised cheek, bruised

        mouth and chin, dark red

bruising about her lips . . .

    Fine bruises
on back   flanks   abdomen;

            pinkish, pinky-orange bruises
      symmetrical on both shoulders

        which might represent   *grip marks.*

    Bruising, deep
in the soft tissue of the face . . . bruising

       down to the skull bone, yes.

A word like sediment, layer
        upon layer. Blood
                slowed, sullen
                        stilled.

    The colours in the photographs so mottled
the Crown asked

        Are these colours true?

5.

    The head, when shaven:

... a textured pattern ...
        suggestive of the sole of a running shoe ...

6.

    The pathologist's hands, along

the throat's interior
    the tongue, the bone below.

    Hands moving in the mouth.
        A woman's hands. A girl's mouth.

Hands. Force. Law. At times she spoke of Reena
    as she might

someone she knew, someone living.

        A healthy young woman, she said.

    Other times she spoke as though the body
could say what it wanted.

    There are different kinds of shock

        but I think in her case it would be a desire
        to save herself.

Skin

It wasn't said. What we were, beneath the skin of our respectability.
My father, a doctor, his accent learned from Indians who studied
in England. My mother, a Mary Kay consultant: pink makeup kits
in the living room, the paperback success story on her night table.
How I dreamed of her winning the pink fur-trimmed coat,
the pink Cadillac.

Unsaid, as she held my brother's hand, going door to door to find
out who had beaten him with a bag full of bottles. Her wrist
a golden ribbon between the gap of coat sleeve and glove.

~

Once I woke in the morning and looked out my window to see
boot prints in fresh snow. A trampled path, as though someone had
take a shortcut through our backyard, suddenly unsure which way
to go. As though I'd rubbed my eyes too hard, opened them again
to see dark stains on the light. An afterimage. The watermark
on my grandfather's stationery.

I went outside in my nightgown and winter boots. Stomped it
out, beat my arms, did a little chicken dance of fury and shame.
Paki. I wasn't even — A word, mouthed in snow.

~

I perfected my English. That is not what I am. I wasn't even
from there, didn't speak that language, was not dark brown like
the servants, *les bonnes* who cleaned our house, the chauffeur,
the gardener, the tailor "back home," Bhai Aziz, Bhai Yousouf,
Shiva. Did not carry the bitter scent of turmeric on my skin,
the smoky rose of agarbhatti; did not glisten with the shine of
almond oil and sweat. That is not what I am. That is not what
I am. I perfected my English.

Tillicum Bridge

On the underside of Tillicum
I turn my back to the water

        lace fingers through chain-link
           to look at stone

where they found

        fire-altered rock, ash and charcoal...
          shell remains from oysters,
             mussels, clams and crabs...

(a fence around natural stone
        as though stone might turn feral)

Four thousand years old

...the bones of fish, deer and seals...
    fragments left
        from the making of stone tools...

Middens, tells, the archaeologist said

        (*tell*, a word from Arabic, from Hebrew

a site that holds evidence
        of successive human occupation

to untell, to uncover the layers
    of this evidence

to retell, to try to restore the site
to its original state)

...herring, salmon, a variety of birds...

Each site an event
destroyed by the process
through which we read it
broken strata

ruined interrelation of artifacts

site loss

Still we read
*red, oxidized earth
scorched rock, fire-cracked rock*

the wrecking-ball wisdom of archaeology

things can only be uncovered

once

Craigflower Bridge

Get up.

A bridge is wood trestle below, metal
above; a guardrail

of teal-green lattice. Hennaed patches of rust.
"I need help. I need help. I need help."

A bridge is a distance, measured in steps, in pools
of lamplight, the time it takes to cross.

In breaths. — *How far did you watch her go?*
— *Halfway across, to where the light spreads out.*

Headlights of passing cars, bright beads on a wire
that curves into darkness: Highway 1A, Gorge Road.

— *Did you observe her gait as she crossed?*
I thought of the gaits of Indian dance,

the little I learned, carrying
my clumsiness far into adulthood:

elephant, peacock, deer. — *She was
staggering, light-headed.*

A bridge is held up by belief that you will go
over to the other shore

to someone who wants you, to somewhere
safe.

To tear with the teeth

— The tide was in, the tide was out, I don't know —
— Why did you tell a lie about the tide?

The sky today, the same faded blue
as my mother's nikkah sari. Clouds like tarnished sequins.
I want to lay down flowers, but it feels intrusive;
instead I walk across the bridge and count my steps.
Downstream, a cormorant dives; I follow it
in mind, a pendant yanked, bubbles a strand of pearls
loosened and scattered. *Gorgeous*, from the old French
for throat, for a stone that adorns the throat.

If something is allowed to flood and recede
and flood again. Twelve years of trials. A childhood.
Notebooks filled with my anxious cursive, *I* like a fishhook
on each line. Why is it so hard
to say it? Guidebooks, passages underlined. *If you run a strand*
of eelgrass through the teeth, it makes a sound like 'hsh'
Heisha-heisha, meaning, *to tear with the teeth.*
It's like it wants to be hushed, Cheryl said.

Halocline: the deeper body of seawater, blue-green,
moving upstream; glassine freshwater flowing down.
In another time it would have been possible to see this:
two waters. The Gorge in its abundance. Meadows of eelgrass.
Algae like drifts of organza, green and reddish bronze. I watch
as a heron stilt-walks in sunlight, spreads blue-grey wings
casting shadows on the water that diminish the glare, show the fish
beneath the surface.

THE POETS

PER BRASK is a professor in the Department of Theatre and Film at the University of Winnipeg where he has taught since 1982. He has published poetry, short stories, drama, translations, interviews, and essays in a wide variety of journals and books. *Frayed Opus for Strings & Wind Instruments* is his fifth volume of poetry co-translated with Patrick Friesen.

NORMAN DUBIE is a Regents professor at Arizona State University. A practitioner of Tibetan Buddhism whose work has been translated into thirty languages, Dubie has been the poetry editor for *The Iowa Review* and the director of the graduate poetry workshop at the University of Iowa. Regularly published in *The New Yorker* and other magazines, Dubie is a highly regarded and widely anthologized poet. He has won the Bess Hokin Award of the Modern Poetry Association and fellowships from The Ingram Merrill Foundation, The John Simon Guggenheim Memorial Foundation, and the National Endowment for the Arts. He lives in Tempe, Arizona.

PATRICK FRIESEN is a poet, essayist, playwright, and translator living in Victoria, B.C. His most recent publications are *jumping in the asylum* (2011), *a dark boat* (2012), and *a short history of crazy bone* (2015). He has co-translated five volumes of poetry with Per Brask.

ULRIKKA S. GERNES was born in 1965 in Sweden to Danish parents. At the age of twenty-two she moved to Copenhagen, Denmark, already a published and highly acclaimed poet. Her first collection, *Natsvoermer*, was published in Denmark in 1984, when she was eighteen years old. Since then she has published an additional ten collections, all of them received gratefully in the Danish press. She is also the author of two books for children, as well as many short stories, songs, and various contributions to literary anthologies, art catalogues, magazines, newspapers, and Danish National radio.

JOY HARJO is an internationally known performer and writer of the Mvskoke/Creek Nation, the author of ten books of poetry and, most recently, a memoir, *Crazy Brave*. A critically acclaimed poet, her many honours include a Guggenheim Fellowship, the Josephine Miles Poetry Award, the William Carlos Williams Award, and the American Indian Distinguished Achievement in the Arts Award. She lives in Tulsa, Oklahoma.

LIZ HOWARD was born and raised in northern Ontario. She received an Honours Bachelor of Science with High Distinction from the University of Toronto. Her poetry has appeared in Canadian literary journals such as *The Capilano Review*, *The Puritan*, and *Matrix Magazine*. Her chapbook *Skullambient* was shortlisted for the bpNichol Chapbook Award. She recently completed an MFA in Creative Writing through the University of Guelph and works as a research officer in cognitive psychology at the University of Toronto.

DON PATERSON was born in Dundee, Scotland, in 1963. His previous poetry collections include *Nil Nil*, *God's Gift to Women*, *Landing Light*, and *Rain*. He has also published two books of aphorisms, as well as translations of Antonio Machado and Rainer Maria Rilke. His poetry has won many awards, including the Whitbread Poetry Prize, the Geoffrey Faber Memorial Prize, and all three Forward Prizes; he is currently the only poet to have won the T.S. Eliot

Prize twice. He was awarded the Queen's Gold Medal for Poetry in 2009. He is a Fellow of the Royal Society of Literature, the English Association, and the Royal Society of Edinburgh, and is currently Professor of Poetry at the University of St. Andrews. Since 1997 he has been poetry editor at Picador Macmillan, and he also works as a jazz musician and composer. He lives in Edinburgh.

SORAYA PEERBAYE's first collection of poetry, *Poems for the Advisory Committee on Antarctic Names*, was nominated for the Gerald Lampert Award. Her poems have appeared in *Red Silk: An Anthology of South Asian Women Poets* (2004), edited by Priscila Uppal and Rishma Dunlop, as well as the literary journals *Other Voices*, *Prairie Fire*, and *The New Quarterly*; she has also contributed to the chapbook anthology *Translating Horses*. She holds an MFA in Creative Writing from the University of Guelph. She lives in Toronto with her husband and daughter.

ROWAN RICARDO PHILLIPS is the author of *Heaven* (2015) and *The Ground* (2012). He is the recipient of a Whiting Writers' Award, the PEN/Joyce Osterweil Award, the GLCA New Writers Award for Poetry, and a Guggenheim Fellowship. He lives in New York City.

THE JUDGES

ALICE OSWALD has published six collections of poetry and selected poems of both Thomas Wyatt and Ted Hughes. She has won several awards, including the T.S. Eliot, Ted Hughes, Hawthornden, Cholmondley, and Warwick. She works part time as a gardener and performs widely.

TRACY K. SMITH is the author of three acclaimed books of poetry: *The Body's Question*, winner of the Cave Canem Poetry Prize; *Duende*, winner of the James Laughlin Award of the Academy of American Poets and an Essence Literary Award; and, most recently, *Life on Mars*, winner of the 2012 Pulitzer Prize, a *New York Times* Notable Book, a *New York Times Book Review* Editors' Choice, and a *New Yorker, Library Journal*, and *Publishers Weekly* Best Book of the Year. Other honours include a Wallace Stegner Fellowship, a Rona Jaffe Foundation Writers' Award, a Whiting Writers' Award, and an Academy of American Poets Fellowship. She is a professor of Creative Writing at Princeton University.

ADAM SOL has published four collections of poetry, the latest of which, *Complicity*, was released in 2014. His previous collections include *Jeremiah, Ohio*, a novel in poems that was shortlisted for Ontario's Trillium Award for Poetry; *Crowd of Sounds*, which won the award in 2004; and *Jonah's Promise*. He has published fiction, scholarly essays, and reviews for a variety of publications, including the *Globe and Mail, Lemon Hound*, and *Joyland.com*. He teaches at Laurentian University's campus in Barrie, Ontario, and lives in Toronto with his wife, Rabbi Yael Splansky, and their three sons.

ACKNOWLEDGEMENTS

The publisher thanks the following for their kind permission to reprint the work contained in this volume:

"Prologue Speaking in Tongues," "British Petroleum," "The Novel as Manuscript," "Lines for Little Mila," "The Quotations of Bone," "At First Sky in April," "Under a Tabloid Moon," and "The Mirror" from *The Quotations of Bone* by Norman Dubie are reprinted by permission of Copper Canyon Press.

"We Were There When Jazz Was Invented," "Talking With the Sun," "Spirit Walking in the Tundra," "Midnight is a horn player," "Charlie and the Baby," and "Sunrise" from *Conflict Resolution for Holy Beings* by Joy Harjo are reprinted by permission of W.W. Norton & Company.

"Wave," "Lacrima," "Francesca Woodman," "The Version," "Requests," "For a Drowned Poet," "Mercies," and "The Roundabout" from *40 Sonnets* by Don Paterson are reprinted by permission of Faber and Faber.

"Kingdom Come," "Little Song," *Measure for Measure*, "Lucas and Mark," "The Beatitudes of Malibu," and "The Once and Future King of Ohio" from *Heaven* by Rowan Ricardo Phillips are reprinted by permission of Farrar, Straus and Giroux.

"A frayed opus for strings," "Night-black silver, January's luminous," "K was supposed to come with the key, I was," "Barely five minutes later we've moved into," "I have to find F. I don't know why and I don't know," "In the thicket of possibilities I choose the continental," "On H.C. Andersen Boulevard during rush hour," and "No more now. Even fear has fear. Even of itself." from *Frayed Opus for Strings & Wind Instruments* by Per Brask and Patrick Friesen, translated from the Danish written by Ulrikka S. Gernes.

"Boreal Swing," "Standard Time," "A Wake," "Debarker," "Henceforth, Through the Forest," "Bigger Than," and "North by South" from *Infinite Citizen of the Shaking Tent* by Liz Howard are reprinted by permission of McClelland & Stewart.

"Trials," "Autopsy," "Skin," "Tillicum Bridge," "Craigflower Bridge," and "To tear with the teeth" from *Tell: poems for a girlhood* by Soraya Peerbaye are reprinted by permission of Pedlar Press.

THE GRIFFIN POETRY PRIZE
Anthology 2016

The best books of poetry published in English internationally and in Canada are honoured each year with the $65,000 Griffin Poetry Prize, one of the world's most prestigious and richest literary awards. Since 2001 this annual prize has acted as a tremendous spur to interest in and recognition of poetry, focusing worldwide attention on the formidable talent of poets writing in English and works in translation. And each year the editor of *The Griffin Poetry Prize Anthology* gathers the work of the extraordinary poets shortlisted for the awards, and introduces us to some of the finest poems in their collections.

This year, editor and prize juror Adam Sol's selections from the international shortlist include poems from Norman Dubie's *The Quotations of Bone* (Copper Canyon Press), Joy Harjo's *Conflict Resolution for Holy Beings* (W.W. Norton & Company), Don Paterson's *40 Sonnets* (Faber and Faber), and Rowan Ricardo Phillips's *Heaven* (Farrar, Straus and Giroux). The selections from the Canadian shortlist include poems from Per Brask and Patrick Friesen's *Frayed Opus for Strings & Wind Instruments* (Brick Books), translated from the Danish written by Ulrikka S. Gernes, *Infinite Citizen of the Shaking Tent* by Liz Howard (McClelland & Stewart), and *Tell: poems for a girlhood* by Soraya Peerbaye (Pedlar Press).

In choosing the 2016 shortlist, prize jurors Alice Oswald, Tracy K. Smith, and Adam Sol each read 633 books of poetry, from 43 countries, including 25 translations. The jury also wrote the citations that introduce the seven poets' nominated works. Royalties generated from *The Griffin Poetry Prize Anthology 2016* will be donated to UNESCO's World Poetry Day, which was created to support linguistic diversity through poetic expression and to offer endangered languages the opportunity to be heard in their communities.